Essex Clay

ANDREW MOTION

FABER & FABER

First published in 2018
by Faber & Faber Ltd
Bloomsbury House
74–77 Great Russell Street
London WC1B 3DA
This paperback edition first published in 2019

Typeset by Hamish Ironside
Printed in the UK by TJ International Ltd, Padstow, Cornwall

A CIP record for this book is available from the British Library

ISBN 978-0-571-33997-6

ESSEX CLAY

Gillian Motion 1928–1978

and

Richard Motion 1921–2006

Acknowledgements

Acknowledgements and thanks are due to *The Echo Chamber* (BBC Radio 4), on which a part of this poem was broadcast in December 2017.

Contents

ESSEX CLAY

PART ONE

The intact frost of early morning
     and a blade of ice
          drawn from the tap in the stable yard.

The village as they drive through
               half asleep under twisting chimneys.

The church   Victorian Doomsday
     moored to the hilltop edge
          with its pretty flotilla of graves.

The weathervane cockerel's gold and flying eye.

The lane
     straightening beside water meadows
          under a thatch of bare chestnuts
               shattered with daylight.

Gravel in the ford
          washed by the brimming stream
     the Blackwater
and pebbles magnified   tawny   beach colours
     with that other river   the river of shining tar
          shivering underneath.

Last night's snowdust
     in suddenly wide-open ploughed fields.

     Flints like hip bones and knee bones.

          Clay clods supporting
miniature drift-triangles on their windward side.

His mother silent beside him
        her yellow hair trapped and placid in a hairnet

her clean cream jodhpurs   red collar   black riding jacket

        her stock like a bandage

            her gold pin
                adorned with the mask of a fox.

                        *

He is seventeen   confident   opinionated
                and definitely at odds
                                on this subject at least.

        He does not approve.

    But   when he glances into the footwell
and sees his mother's narrow feet
                fluffy sheepskin slippers
                paddling by turns at the brake
                    accelerator   clutch
        he is silent.

He cannot bring himself
            to have that argument again.

                        *

    In the car park of the White Hart
                    also the bus stop
he reminds himself

    [6]

no one makes a scene   not at his age

and condescends   tips his head a little
     to kiss his mother goodbye.

A skim of skin
    is enough.

But he does see and cannot forget her hairnet in close-up
   a black cobweb   tougher of course

   and feels it
     scratch
       the tip of his nose.

Then he is out in the wind buttoning his overcoat
   the ankle-length   topsoil-brown   itchy
      war-time soldier's greatcoat
       the British Warm
       borrowed from his father's wardrobe
  without permission
      stolen actually
which makes him   beside his holdall
    a soldier himself
     he imagines.

*

Exactly as his mother grinds the Hillman back into gear
   the silhouette of his bus
     bulges over the hilltop beyond the White Hart.

He flinches away
   to discover his mother's face is

already no longer her face
but an after-image
hovering a little way behind her
as she guns the engine   and wriggles into
the traffic flow.

Her exhaust plume rapidly fades into the spectre of
a spectre.

Dark petrol-dribbles escaping the pipe
might well be a trail of crumbs
dot-dot-dot all the way home.

*

The bus is almost past him now   except
when he hoists his arm
the whole snow-filthy bulk amazingly

stops.

Double doors hiss open.

Cigarette fug flops out.

And in he steps
with too many hands
or not enough hands
to pay the fare
to manage the bloody holdall
to hold   tight.

It's OK sonny it's OK.

Twirling up to the top deck
      stumbling as the bus surges and sashays
        forward
          with a shudder through every one of its
           body plates
he lurches for a last glimpse of the lane back to the
  village
    and finds no car in sight.

                 *

From this height
    smearing the window mist with his sleeve
      the whiskery sleeve that makes an O
    fringed with delicate nettle-hair scratch marks
he can see across a whole cabbage field
    creased with snow.

      And no one the entire journey
  to notice even   let alone ridicule
    either the relief
      or the alarm of solitude
he reveals by leaning his head against the glass
      on the trembling chill
  and pretending he is asleep.

Although   despite appearances
   he is still watching in fact   vaguely
the shadow of the bus shrink
    where it meets a burst of heavy snow
      then elongate as the snow weakens

so one minute he sees himself not at all
    the next topples forward across hedgerows
    brick walls
        window panes
            cars shawled at the curbside
                shop fronts   mannequins
                    slopes of threadbare winter wheat

and below this the clay six feet deep
        malevolent pasty face
           ash smears and ochre
a dead weight but in fact alive
    sluggishly
           waiting with all the time in the world
to sculpt its lead around gumboots and plough blades
                to rear and obliterate whatever it can

until an hour has gone and the bus flusters
        into Sawbridgeworth
           where its shadow abruptly
    falls in through the windows and sinks down
        among the other shadows already assembled
           and is absorbed.

*

Clambering out
        holdall thumping the door
he forgets himself
    the instant he sets eyes upon her.

Juliet.

    Her face and love-name coinciding.

Her black hair   black
         not a black enough word.

         Her red mouth.

      Her skin white   but mainly full
         ripeness.

And she is looking straight at him.

      She is.

         Glittering and
      ignoring her fluttery mother beside her
which he should not.

      He shakes her mother's hand
headscarf   specs   face-fuzz powder.

      But for Juliet

         their cheeks brush-collide
and he smells
               mint.

      Should have thought of that.

Never mind.
               Just find the car
                  boot tricky
                  crammed already
with a clutch of decapitated shopping-bag fledglings.

      It's OK sonny it's OK.

Then next question.

Front seat or back.

Back.

But hunching forward   laying one forearm flat
        on pale-green clammy plastic
Juliet's black hair a swelling wave
        trapped inside her collar
                until they set off

                and the heater cranks up

and Juliet
            slips her hand
        inside this wave of black to set it free
            and it flood-slithers
over the shoulders of her coat onto his hand
        which jolts in the electric shock.

                        *

        Afternoon   already   somehow
and Juliet's mother has disappeared thank you God
            she has work to do
        while   despite the cold
the clouds and snow flurries
        shovelling west from Siberia
            he and Juliet leave the house for a walk.

He spares a thought for his own mother.

Will she be home already
                defeated
she would say that
                defeated
                        by cold.

Her voice stays with him through the back yard
        ghosting

                        boiler shed
ghosting
                        dog kennel
ghosting
                        wood shed
ghosting.

        But he cannot hear what the ghost says.

                        *

They step from the lee of the house
                immediately into ice puffs
where cold slits his eyes

        and he sees ahead   guesses rather
a dead prairie sprinkled with snowstones
                his greatcoat
                        not so ridiculous now

        no more than Juliet's white fur hat and
Afghan or   Doctor Zhivago number
        fur blustering at collar and wrists
                while she butts into the wind

                                        [13]

arms folded tight   hugging herself
one blue vein pulsing in her porcelain neck.

*

As for his own face
     he cannot   dare not
   what with eyes streaming   whole face
stiff like a stroke   but still
   blathering   this and that
     this and that
   their destination of all things
next year's Christmas trees
    dimly darkening the horizon.

*

Well
    they do ask for it farmers
   ripping everything out
hedges   hundreds of years
   shelter.

*

And yet he still does manage
to lead her on.

As she leads him
down the long narrow headland

[14]

snowflakes glued on the winter wheat shoots
dithering beside them.

*

Jesus though
laughable this cold
laughable and
suddenly it gets the better of him.

So he veers
leaf blown
back the way they came.

But Juliet is deliberately standing in his way.

And his mouth
did she mean this
obviously she meant this
his mouth
blurs runnily back to life in the warmth of her mouth.

For a moment there is

pure darkness.

Pure slippery deepening wet dark.

And heat
as his hand slides inside her coat.

Astounding radiator heat.

When he touches bare skin
        between the waist of her jeans and her jersey
and Juliet slides her mouth from his mouth to his ear
        where she pours into him
                the blaze of his own name.

                                *

                He wants her now.

He wants her
        among the snowdropped wheat tips
and flints
        gleaming between the seed drills.

        In the slicing snow swipes.

Under the weightless silk cloud sheet.

                A perfectly ridiculous idea.

Although
        when they bow towards the house
                arms looping each other's shoulders
against the wind opposing
        they realise   what they have promised each other.

                                *

There is an hour before they must change
                                        for the party.

Juliet insists
they have to go.

After she has dragged the curtains shut
after she has lit the fire
after she has flicked through her box of LPs and
chosen
Music from Big Pink

soul mate

he stands to one side of the room by the curtains
a proper   young   man
beside the floor-length wall-to-wall expensive blue
velvet curtains
with snow falling outside
and agrees.

Of course they must.

He stares flagrantly at her in the armchair
to show he would rather not.

Knees drawn up   legs curled round like
a mermaid on a rock

not that

like herself
right hand shielding her eyes
concentrating on 'The Weight'
I pulled in to Nazareth
left hand   square-tipped fingers

tightening round her bare ankle
              and the little vein mesh there
        the blood delta
              pale lavender.

                         *

        When he has made his point
he collects and removes himself to the spare room
              as ordered
the soft-lit   oak-panelled
              low-ceilinged spare room.

        Here he prepares himself.

    He takes time
          shaking out creases
    from his new white shirt with the jabot collar.

    He sounds   with all he dares of his weight
              the nervous springs in the high bed.

    He begins to imagine

              or will it be her room.

                         *

A knock
          the polite wood-knuckle sort.

    Juliet.

Has she   what
          has she
changed her mind.

Is it now.

Then the door creaks and
          he sees not Juliet
Juliet's mother
          and the look of her makes his smile
                    stiffen.

He thinks
                    is she
          peering into his head.

          Is she   about to forbid.

But that would not explain why
          she is crying.

    It would not explain why
          she is wiping tears from both eyes
pinching her nose as if she might sneeze
          dimpling the eiderdown with her fingertips
                    the silvery blue eiderdown
                    stitched into lumpy waves
to occupy herself with the patterns she makes.

                    *

    A grown woman
          talking as she is crying.

Like suffocation.

        But she does say clearly enough
      methodical for a moment at least
   his father has called on the telephone.

His father has called
       and his father.

     He interrupts.

With the inspiration of dread
       a mind-burst
    like a sapling
twigs   branches   quick green flickering
     instantly becoming a tree
        he tells her   he already knows
          what she has to say.

And true
    there is nothing like surprise in his voice.

    Brain juddering.

        Turbulence.

   But even that soon settles down
the air he breathes becoming perfectly smooth and
   steady again
      and him dry-eyed

at one remove from himself admittedly
    watching himself
as Juliet's mother tells him

squinting at her watch
      restraining the frilly white cuff of her blouse

his mother now
      just exactly now in fact
            as they are speaking

his mother is in surgery because

      she is still not looking at him
          she is still studying her watch

his mother is in surgery at St John's Hospital in
   Chelmsford
      where his father has already arrived.

Because of the accident   he tells her impatiently
      and wants to add
            but does not add
      takes pity on her
          as she backs away to the door
      both hands covering her mouth
adds to himself at least

      he has expected this all his life
feared would be better
      he has feared this all his life
and the only surprising thing
      but he cannot say this
      the only surprising thing is

      he wants to know more than anything
          where Juliet is
the corridor   her room   waiting

not waiting any more
how could she be
waiting
or him
how could he wait for her
after this.

*

But they do go to the party.

It is explained
he cannot return home
there is no one

and his father
Juliet's mother says
his father thinks the party will stop him

what

worrying.

He doubts very much
worrying is the word
and that
is another thing he will not say.

Instead
he will do as his father wants.

He will   because of this
        seizing the new word   new to him
                injury.

                        *

    He tries it again under his breath
            injury
when Juliet's mother ushers him
            injury
    and Juliet out of her car at the party
        then spins away
            in a red-flare exhaust-ghost snow-flap

        relieved
        he understands

while he and Juliet
    not escaping the icy lunge
        of a magnolia hand by the front door
            injury
so he is soaked along the left arm of his new white shirt
        the shirt his father hates

while he and Juliet
            duck into this stranger's house
        he thinks might not even exist
except as a stack of crammed and shining rooms
    bolted together with injury
        with bars of very loud music.

                        *

In the emptied-out dance room

empty apart from the Stonehenge sideboard
        which will never be the same again
                after that fag-end gouging a ruby furrow

in the space-trip spangling disco ball light

        in the profound heat
                and rock-thrash

he must tell everyone
        he has this new distinction
    at the top of his lungs if necessary.

His mother is dying   probably
        even as he stands here.

        His mother is dying.

But the room   the entire house
    decides this is not important
            and the music drowns it.

The music   the dancing
    the talk of nothing
                of everything but.

Juliet will not have it either.

        She is under orders
        and motherly a bit.

He must be cheerful
he must be occupied
he must be distracted.

So

here she is now   refilling his drink
here she is now   introducing him
here she is now   mouthing his name
here she is now   finding a side room
and settling herself   onto his knee
on both knees now   in his lap
with her   slippery weight and heat
moulding him through the dusk-red
satin trousers she has made herself

and

in the run-up to midnight
after someone has dimmed the lights

in the maze of a slow song

fatuous lyrics   he can hear that   fatuous
but who cares

laying her long bare arms on his shoulders
allowing him to breathe
the sleepy vanilla scent in the crease of her elbows
linking her fingers behind his neck
resting her forehead on his forehead
her black hair
her skin sealed to his skin

as if her thoughts could fill him
                as if she could flood him
with the perfect blank of her superior happiness.

                              *

It is embarrassing
                or something
when they slither into the deep cracked back seat
        of her mother's Rover
because at midnight sharp she has come to collect them.

He wishes the meat of his neck and shoulders
        were bruised by the weight of Juliet's arms.

He wishes his whole body had scorched
        when she nested on his knees
                in her sleek satin.

He wishes his mind had received her mind
        like a lake swallowing the stream that feeds it.

He wishes.

                And yet.

Although they are leaning together holding hands
        welded in the sublunary capsule of the car
he discovers after a mile or two
        Juliet is not noticeable to him.

        Not really.

Not compared to the silence
        hardening between the three of them
as witch trees weave their way home into a tunnel.

Not compared to the doubly darkened air
        sharpening polar blue dots
                and pin-prick foxy eyes
in the fuel gauge and speedometer.

Not compared to Juliet's mother sparking a cigarette
        then milling open her window
                the smoke tugged outside
                        like a streak of chalk
while at the same time
        allowing shavings of the night flying past them

to curl in
        pure   sharp

despite the blurry cigarette whiff
        which he discovers
gives him a feeling of drowning
        of sinking below the frozen surface of the world
but also of rising
        of becoming a ghost himself

until   when he turns his head
                now ignoring Juliet entirely
he sees in the tunnel of the lane behind them
        in the tail lights
where gravel flares under the narrowing branches

a wreckage trail
                    made of his mother's possessions
              her riding jacket   her red collar
              her jodhpurs   her sheepskin slippers
              her Teasmade   her *Ring of Bright Water*
              her pair of pretend tortoiseshell hairbrushes
                         and mirror
              her stock   her gold pin with the fox mask
              her black velvet hard hat
her whole wardrobe of everything in fact
                    not much for a life
vanishing along with the moment he sees it
                    as the pasty clay hand stretches
from underground and grabs.

                              *

The Rover whooshes in
        between what must once have been gateposts
the gate itself long gone
              as Juliet's mother flicks her cigarette
out through the window crack
              and winds the handle backwards.

The cold stops at once.

The snow
              slows down.

The snowflakes in the headlights
        cleverly assemble
              into a swivelling cone
                    centred exactly on him.

He deliberately resists
        their attempt at hypnosis.

He sees the cigarette bounce once on the gravel
        fizz
                and shrink to a glowering red eye
                        that keeps watching.

                                    *

When Juliet's mother has parked her car in the garage

when he has climbed out
        into the rank petrol stink
                the suicidal exhaust fumes

when he has negotiated
        the child's sleigh   spare tyre
                Flit spray   garden hose
festooning the walls

when they have slithcred in from the snow blast
                to the shimmering kitchen

Juliet's mother reminds him he must be tired
        recommends Juliet to fetch him a glass of water
                and tramps upstairs
thinking she is doing him and Juliet a favour.

Her door eases shut at the far end
        of the long brown top-landing carpet with a sober
        click
                and he thinks no more about her.

He thinks almost nothing.

He has no room for anything.

He notices   instead.

He notices

from the wicker dog basket
          creaks
as the dog   they have hardly been introduced
     a black Labrador
               sidles in from the hallway
          rotates once
and flops

     clock ticks
          from the moronic moon face
                    beaming above the Aga

     house plant
               aspidistra is it   keep that
flying then
          stiff green flag shreds

     water
          the glass Juliet has brought him
misting on the kitchen table
     while he rubs the side of his thumb to and fro
          across the hysterical woodgrain
years of scrubbing have exposed as ridges

     Juliet
          leaning the small of her back against the sink
head down   face streaked by hair fallen forward again

shoes off
        stretching her toes.

This silence   he thinks
        this silence
but he cannot complete the thought.

    A minute later
he drinks a mouthful of the water.

Another minute
    he says good night and retreats upstairs.

*

The moon peers at him
    over her neat cloud fold
and decides   it is time to change her orbit.

    She swings closer to the Earth.

    She whispers to him
in a white voice like ice fixing grass
    that now she has taken over the duties of the sun.

    That her bright light
        will shine by day
as well as by night.

    And he accepts this.

He turns his face upwards
    and spreads his arms as wide as possible.

The moon in sympathy
         rests her entire weight
    on the shell of his chest.

He embraces her and
         she absorbs him.

                  He feels nothing at all.

                        *

Next morning the bus station is deserted.

    In the front seat of Juliet's mother's car he waits.

He asks himself
    what does the back of his head look like
         to Juliet behind him
    and has no idea.

              He waits.

    He breathes on the windscreen
              until gradually   patchily
         the mist tide retreats.

              He waits.

He thinks the concrete walls of the bus station sparkle
    or is that his imagination.

              He waits.

Certainly in his imagination
        he sees the Earth dangling
clear in the frost of its fatal winter
        in its epic and eternal lack of deliberate intent
        its brainless habit   not even habit
condition
        its condition of perpetual accident.

            He waits.

And when his bus eventually fusses into the station
        under the almost-too-low dry-blood-coloured steel
            girder
and other passengers materialise from the supermarket
    adjacent
        and from High Street patting snow off their over-
            coats
            he makes his goodbye.

            Not a kiss

        an embrace sort of for Juliet
            twisting over the seat dividing them

and for her mother a handshake
        which she rejects
briskly negotiating the steering wheel
        to smother then fling him away
            bundling his holdall after.

The car door behind him slams shut
        as the double door of the bus

                opens.

He steps towards it   the exact fare ready in his fist
        and the collar of his army greatcoat up round his
            ears
                tickling a bit.

No need to show that.

Keep going
            OK.

                Pay
                    OK.

                    Turn OK
                        and wave.

                    *   *   *

In the car park of the White Hart
a neighbour   Mrs Hill   is waiting for him
      boxy in her boxy Land Rover.

He is thinking   if he is thinking
      the same as yesterday.

      Snow on the wind.

Glittering gravel glued together by frost.

The pub sign
      wincing in its frame.

Wham   wham   wham
      shuddering past on the A120.

Even the darker skewed tyre tracks
      carved by his mother's Hillman
            still present and correct.

At least Mrs Hill does not ask him
      how was the party.
                  She avoids that pothole.

      Also   she has no idea about Juliet
and he will not say.

However   what can she tell him about his mother.

As Mrs Hill twists the ignition key
      hunches over the steering wheel
            and they kangaroo forward

she manages   mostly
     to keep control of the matter-of-fact voice
          she has evidently rehearsed all morning.

His father has rung to tell her
what the others had told him
since he himself saw nothing.

His mother's pony Serenade
was jumping out of a copse.

She pecked. His mother fell.

She injured   she injured
her head   and she lay
unconscious.

               An ambulance
ferried her away to St John's.

Today she is still unconscious
after the operation last night.

He will understand of course
he cannot visit her   yet.

               His father thinks
that would not be a good idea.

He nods his own head   something is making him
          but he must
     why not visit her.

Mrs Hill delivers her answer
    as they curve down from the A120
       past the silage clamp
         sulking under its black tarpaulin
           weighed down with tractor tyres
   through the rip of the ford
beneath the chestnuts with snow congealed on their
  fingertips
        and his mind jars open.

     Squat meringue ambulance
     flash light icy blue flash light
     mud concrete track his mother
     hard black velvet riding hat
     flung aside on a plough crest

     his mother high pillow bank
     yellow hair no hair shaved off
     succulent bruise red green-grey
     eyes shut eyes sunk eye sockets
     octopus oxygen mask clamping

     hiss hiss hiss hiss hiss hiss hisssss
     astronaut capsule open weightless
     bare surface dusty surface pebbly
     a planet no one has visited before.

              *

His grandmother is rotating on the front step at home
    waiting to look after him.

To what.

His grandmother approaching eighty
                frail   deaf   incapable
                        utterly perplexed.

                His mother is her daughter.

He reminds himself of this as Mrs Hill disappears
                elated he thinks   like Juliet's mother
                        she has done her bit
                        and his grandmother offers her cheek
                a soft little rag of crumpled linen
                        which irritates him
why   he does not want to think.

Except
        suddenly everything irritates him.

                Everything.

Pink hyacinths his mother propped upright
                with two grey knitting needles
                        nevertheless swooning on the hall table.

TV advertising loudly in the sitting room
        to an audience of large empty chairs.

Swish of the dishwasher
        they never use that and anyway
                why at midday.

Most of all his grandmother's dog Janey
        hideous straw-stuffed overstuffed body
                hideous continual barking
        barking   barking   barking

and   come lunchtime
      when it is tethered by his grandmother
         to the leg of the dining-room table
   still barking   barking and lunging
dragging away the whole table and his plate with it
      as he aims his fork to stab
        cold ham and salad.

*

He pounds upstairs to his bedroom
      and its gloom sanctuary
curtains permanently drawn even before today
      poster of Soft Machine
    glimmering as if it lived for ever
        in the incense flicker of altar lights.

He has decided one thing.

   He has decided to anchor
      everything that remains
in the continual stillness of remembering.

    Therefore
while his grandmother croons to herself in the spare room
      or Janey maybe
  he visits everywhere in the house
and examines objects in their places.

The ancient longways-splitting block of grimy soap
in the downstairs washroom used only by his father.

The picture in the hallway of a horse leaping over
a gate with the gate broken but the gate's shadow not.

The tile in the boot room representing the coat of arms
of the Bishop of Chelmsford for reasons he never
    fathomed.

The front door where at sunset with the temperature
    dropping
ice ticks faintly as it tightens on a puddle under the
    hawthorn.

The darkness   not an object
        it might as well be
the darkness back in his room again   the cube
    of safe air
        he thought it was safe
            the darkness now melting in silky strings
                    and droplets
        becoming atoms   prickling atoms
            buzzing and scooting
                colossal buffetings in nature
            but all mute all
                mute
even the infinitely tall gas flame of his mother's scream
                more silent
            than dust settling on moss.

                    *

Every evening now   seven or seven-thirty
        he loiters in his bedroom
and
        when his father's car leaps into the garage
            after his return from hospital
where he has stopped on the way from work

when the chrysanthemum glare of his headlights
        withers against the back wall

    when his father's immaculate black London shoes
stamp across the tarmac to the front door
    at a military pace

    he slinks down to the hallway.

    He sees his father then
        head and shoulders wavering
through the two glass panels.

My father   he asks himself   my father
        have we met.

    Dark grey London overcoat
            pale grey face
        hair white-grey at the temples
and head bowed under the dome of the outside light.

    Merciless white light
        like the sun of a planet nowhere near to Earth.

His father pauses.

                    His father collects himself.

He pretends to wipe dirt off his shoes.

    Have we met.

Then he squares his shoulders and swoops indoors
        swinging his briefcase and

in a separate plastic bag
a dirty nightie
he extracts with a straight arm
to whizz through to the laundry room
but not before
its chalky talc smell
sweat smell
shit smell
has scribbled its signature
the whole length of the hallway.

*

He is sent back to school.

He finds himself afloat
in a new gravity
thinking about thinking
about living in sadness.

Everyone knows.

Everyone
passes him around and between
like a thousand-year-old
priceless manuscript.

And   despite them all
despite himself
he finds a new occupation.

He becomes Horatio in the spring play.

        Not Hamlet.
Horatio.
        Goodnight sweet prince.

        His mother meanwhile
    still floating herself
among the nebulae and gas clouds
    of her vast unconsciousness
        lands on the moon Pneumonia
where the inhabitants are lotus-eaters
    where they dress in mist
where the delectable music
    of waterfalls plays continuously
where she is welcomed with murmurs of affection
        with kisses
where everyone who lives there
        begs her to stay
    and everyone looking on
from the far horizon of her hospital bedside
        begs her to leave
himself included
    when he is allowed to stand there
        for the first time
    which he understands
    will probably be the last time

while his understudy takes over Horatio.

                        *

Nobody has told him
    his mother has become epileptic.

But he sees for himself
when his mother has hauled herself back towards Earth
and his father allows him to visit
alone this time.

He tramps
an eternity of grey linoleum
with a high polish
hard-looking
but surprisingly cushiony underfoot
left   right   straight
left   right   straight
straight   straight   straight   straight
from the front door of St John's
to her ward in a Victorian block
squeezed between the incinerator and a laundry room
as a temporary solution to overcrowding
a hundred years ago.

He steels himself for a long look
at what he has so far only glimpsed
through a cordon of doctors and equipment.

For her shaved head with the stubble
no longer summery fair.

For the orange and red bruise on her temple
maturing to a dead colour
moleskin   trapped   dusty.

For the oxygen tank chipped silver
like treasure salvaged from a wreck.

For her face
        her chin-sag shark face
gaga   mouth hinged with saliva.

But when he arrives round the last corner
                past the nurses' station
into the long ward
                he sees none of this.

There is   his eyes panic
        there is her bed with her
                is this
with her curtain drawn

        with her floor-length pale blue cotton curtain
                twitching and bulging
and black wires   pulleys
        when he pokes his head through the slit

is this
        yes but pinned down   why
in a scrum
        why
                pinned down with four nurses
five
                and a doctor he must be
white coat
        biro scars above the breast pocket
                all of them trying
trying their utmost to
        weigh her down while her body refuses
                while her whole body leaps
like a trout dying in fresh air
                arching clear of the bed

slamming down
     devilish yellow bubbles now in her mouth
         lungfroth
feet dancing
    hands   smothering something
     or strangling

and
       the one in charge
    stethoscope round his neck
        red face
black-frame glasses knocked off his nose almost
   half twisting round without releasing his weight
not for a second
   staring him straight between the eyes
      bellowing

NOT NOW.

*

Grief
    too little a word
       no spring-lock inside it
primed
    to snap back to its opposite
  the second her eyes open   again.

  Sorrow   the same.

    Rage   the same.

Limbo then   limbo
   and better accept it.

Limbo.

    Better stretch out an idea
of life itself permanently stretched out
      touching its Michelangelo fingertips   just
against the outstretched fingers of death
    and vice versa.

*

In this way
    grief becomes
           the strange contentment
     of living in suffering
        without the possibility
of such unhappiness
     in whatever else
       remains of life.

Grief
      even providing a peculiar pleasure
          sometimes
   like the buzz a mind feels
when a tongue
      slides over a painful tooth.

Grief   whispering
        he will be content
   to live in a mirror-bright shining steel universe
     that can never be altered.

*

For three years the heat and dampness of her hand
      shit stink
          sweat stink
             talcum sweetness
and equally that gargoyle stare
    or her eyelids
        tissue paper
    minuscule knotty purple veins
        fluttering   about to open
          never opening
only a fish dream
      rising to the surface
        to sip the light.

    For three years her beautiful thinness
        bloating into a big belly
    a flagon
pumped with drugs through a murky tube
    darting into the crook of her elbow
      also this other tube
        clear white
    into a hole in her throat
      through a metal ring
    that will not stop reminding him
of a washer on the pipe below the kitchen sink
    now they have taken her oxygen mask away.

For three years her palm skin and foot skin
    hardening into flawless alabaster

      the stifling hospital heat
sandpaper really

or the charcoal hands of the ward clock
            polishing her
whenever his back turns.

        And all the while nurses
    squeaking on their deep black rubber soles
        or nurses speaking very loudly
    checking her pulse
            honestly shouting
with never a reply
        never a word from her
not for his father   not for him
            gripping her hand
        absorbing the heat and dampness
                        which gave him life.

                        *

Then his mother opens her eyes.

    She looks
and the first thing she sees is somebody else's voice
        abandoned on the stony surface of the world
            she is now leaving.

    She picks it up
        and keeps on leaving.

She tries it out
        this battered trumpet
                these complex throat fingerings.

No.

       The voice is not hers.

         She does not recognise it.

      Nobody does
in this new world
           she means old
   where she is opening her rusty mouth.

      It is a husky monotone bass.

A throat wheeze.

      A cobwebbed twilit whisper.

But it will do.

It is good enough to blow strange sounds through.

    To ask   in so many words
       what happened
           what happened.
Can I come home now.

               *

He sits with her every day
    in the evenings his father.

It is their new order.

She speaks to him
        questions him rather
with googly eyes and between sleep-falls
    of disastrous depth and weight.

When he questions her
        her face mystifies.

She remembers light years away
        in miniature
    in a splintering dream tunnel
how he stretched towards her.

Or was that a moment ago
    and no one she knows.

One day he is an infant
    the next he becomes
        the same age as himself.

One day he seizes her attention
    the next his voice signal
        witters into infinite space.

He sits with her every day
    in the evenings his father.

                        *

A priest arrives
    someone his father knows
to conduct the service of the Laying on of Hands.

Behind the blue curtain drawn round his mother's bed
          with as much silence as possible
               in a ward at visiting time
                    which is to say
with continual squawks   laughter   sobbing
          soft stream-murmurs of chat
chair scraping
          and thrashing in the curtains

                    this priest steps forward.

He turns out to be an ordinary man in a suit
          and beneath the dog collar
               a black clerical shirt
          shiny with the impression
               of eternal washings and ironings
and a startling cream and yellow brocaded stole
          he whisks out of nowhere
then drapes around his neck.

He stoops
          and stares with his eyes shut.

He magics a prayer book
          and opens it with both hands
               cradling the floppy crocodile cover.

He murmurs
          as quickly as possible
                    a silver stream tinkling over silver stones
embarrassed perhaps
          or is that devout.

And his mother

        he brings himself to look
just about
        at her blazing naked split-openness

            his mother lifts her face
        and her skin tightens
                her skin shines
        unearthly subcutaneous candle wax light
            as she devotes herself
                to the difficult work
        of concentrating extremely hard
on making her wish come true.

His father meanwhile
            at the foot of the bed
        clasping his hands together at waist height
and forgetting to hide
            as he usually does
        the forefinger he squashed
            in a deckchair as a child
his father bows his head
            to hide his wet eyes
and tears in the creases beneath his eyes
        and whatever he thinks.

For his own part
        he watches
                    still.

He sees   at the appointed moment
        the priest lay aside his prayer book
rest his right hand

                    no press   press his right hand
            no both hands   left piled on right
liver-spotted
        hard onto his mother's forehead
            which burns under the weight
                        and ask God
        to enter her.

Lazarus he thinks
        in the second before
                this really is   more than ever
                intensely embarrassing
        in the second before
                this intense embarrassment
                might be an intervention
                as likely as anything
                to kick-start his mother's rigid body
                a body already dead
                before the mind has left it
                and the heart stops

in other words not.

                                    *

He wheels his mother's stretcher
        out from her ward to a corner of the hospital garden
summer grass yellowish between robust clover clumps
        and they sit quietly together
                as mother and son.

Their talk swerves   they like that
        their talk exists again now   and it swerves

but what holds him
        what he cannot avoid coming back to
is the hospital boiler in the shed opposite

    a shed with the wall facing them replaced
        by a single large sheet of glass
to expose the boiler inside.

A boiler   beautiful in its way
    painted valuable silver
        the deep-chested central drum
        dozens of tubes
        offshoots
        returns
        pipes
        drains
        eruptions
all of them shimmering
        the faces on dials
the luxurious flanks
                the dangling and twining arms

    all of them shining like the entrails of a body
housed and cherished outside that body
        and with no ceremony

as discreetly as possible in fact

        in a backwater garden
where no one in the course of a whole long afternoon
    comes to do so much
        as open a stopcock   or read a gauge
            or polish a drum

simply pursuing its business

        hissing sometimes
emitting occasional clicks and whirrs
      yawning extravagantly

pursuing its business while he and his mother
              meander this way and that
      this way and that in their talk together

       until the light fades

and shadows crawl out of the black grass
      to consume them

       and dew falls

and he has no choice   except to wheel his mother back
      and leave her at her place on the ward.

               *

On Sunday mornings he and his father
        collect his mother
in the Ford Transit christened Billy
        ducking and rolling on the Chelmsford road.

      It is hilarious
terrifying he should say.

No one outside the van could possibly know
    how precarious she is   his mother
       how brittle   how eminently
            smashable

tethered by a flimsy seat belt
      a joke
    in the long shiny-floored metal back of the van
    where   if they braked suddenly

        she would rocket forward
      feet first
   through the shattering windscreen
her brokenness everywhere
          breaking.

   The thought of it keeps them desperate
for the emptiness to stretch
      and last
        all the way home
          with no interruption

     soft fawn club-headed grasses
         curtseying at the curbside

     tyres burbling on sweetly

no interruptions
   except sunlight and tree shadow
     pouncing through the windows

and all the green traffic lights agreeing to let them pass

until they swing off the A120

     the White Hart
     in its childish hollow
     there to the right
     red tile roof

gravel car park
still exactly the same

and slow down through the village
checking the church tower as per
knapped flints flashing their glossy hearts
and bright chalk rims and seams

the village shop Tea Rooms
the old Red Lion   now Rufus Leo a house
always worth a smile

pass the tonsure of the new golf course

and so reach the turning circle
the whispery tarmac outside the front door

and stop

in the blunt shade of the empty extension
built at great cost
where the nurse never
where his mother never

and unload his mother onto the van's tail-lift
squealing under her weight
engine grudging
but up to the job just

while a breeze across the ponies' field frisking
the chestnut tree
the tree with the downward-swooping branch
and patch of shiny bark
where Serenade scratches her back

while a breeze
        flaps away the talcum smell
                nearly

    and he and his father
            inch   squeeze
fiddle his mother's stretcher
        through the front door just
                very tight
                        breathe in
they say it every time
                        breathe in
        to the hallway and then with a lah-di-dah
make a laugh of it
                    four-point turn
            enter the sitting room

park her by the fireside
            busily shuffle up a side table
                    set her orange juice there
her pill-bottle battalion

            then   whoosh
                deflate on the sofa
and prepare to talk.

                        *

        He conducts an experiment.

Leaving at the end of visiting hour
        he hammers with his heels
                on the exploding-flower-head carpet tiles

of the corridor to the car park
and sees their blooms
shrivel a little
under the assault of his weight.

He makes as much racket as he decently can
clearing his throat
calling goodbye to the nurses
whistling a merry tune
so his mother will think him gone.

Then he tiptoes back
and peeps round the doorframe.

He sees
which he expects and dreads equally
her head sunk down
on her wafery breastbone.

He sees her eyes
not shut   her eyes blank
blind blue discs
like a statue staring.

He sees her
not herself.

Not present in herself.

He sees her willing herself
to drop through
the detestably tough skin of the world.

*

With no warning

after an arithmetic of years
        he has no reason to think
                are about to become the final amount

pneumonia visits his mother again.

        Pneumonia is a sly one he knows that.

                Pneumonia introduces itself
        as his mother's old friend.

It slips in at her mouth
        when none of the doctors are looking
and curls up inside her
        comfortable as a pussycat dozing.

Then it wakes up and he hears it.

        The growling catarrh.

But his mother.

When he looks into her eyes
        nothing looks back at him.

        She has already heard the delicious promises
                and fallen for them
                        why not
                after a very long time.

She has already seen the radiant centre of the world
        where she is free to rise again
                exactly as needed.

As for him
        he thinks he understands completely.

He thinks for the time being
        there is nothing more he can say.

*   *   *

He remembers   at his mother's funeral

while he is watching his father at her graveside
    his father with smears of Essex clay
        yellowing the heels of his highly polished shoes

his mother telling him
    when his father was a child himself
daydreaming in his bedroom one white afternoon
    he hooked his feet underneath his metal bed rail
        rested his elbows on his knees
           cupped his chin in his hands
so that when his feet slipped and his hands shot upwards
        snapping his mouth shut
    he bit off the tip of his tongue.

What else could he do
        he remembers his mother continuing
    what else could he then do but spit it out
      and carry it carefully downstairs
to his own mother in the kitchen
      and explain what had happened.

And what else could she do
    but drive to the doctor and ask him
      to sew it on again.

      To save the tongue and make it good as new.

PART TWO

Since they buried his mother
his father has moved   two hundred yards
and gone to ground himself
in the humid labyrinth fox-earth of a farm cottage
defended by beech hedge fortifications.

He has retired from human friendships
and grown close
to television.

He has poled himself with his ashplant
thumb cocked in the polished cleft
through every conceivable weather
most tellingly rain
to the churchyard and bowed his head
with the same bafflement at her grave
as the empty grass gap waiting beside it.

In this way thirty years have passed
twenty-eight to be precise
and now his patience has been rewarded.

His father has eaten his breakfast
of one soft-boiled egg and white toast soldiers
balanced a mug of tea into his study
and begun what he has to say.

*

In the bedroom of a house in north London
        he is dressing after a shower
            watching as it happens
                dreaming really
        how January daylight gaining strength
            seems to flex

        to roll in subtle almost-invisible waves
            between the lime tree branches
black lime tree branches spotted with white fungus
            latticing his window.

When the telephone rings
        the definite note in his father's voice
            takes him aback.

Bone cancer   his father announces
        shouting softly into the receiver
            poised a good three inches
                away from his mouth.

It is for him a confident start
        but leads nowhere.

A moment later his father has braked hard
        and peers
                        teeteringly
            over the cliff edge of his own news.

In the pause
        in the ethereal
                crackling
                    vertiginous
            air corridor that opens between them

he imagines his father
                    like a soldier on point
      whose duty is to reconnoitre
            hostile territory ahead.

He pictures him
      frowning over his desktop
            cleared for battle except
                    there is still the question
            of his violated pink blotter
                    with its cryptic mirror writing.

      Over the front lawn
            crew-cut to a bristling softness.

      Over the clenched metallic stubs of rose bushes
                    in two symmetrical beds.

      Over the beech hedge
            wintering as scraps
                    of mysteriously blank brown paper litter
                          skewered on twigs.

      Over the lane
            where car tyres have battered a loaf
                    of green horse dung into the gravel.

      Over the stubble field and ragtag crows
            picking through the remains
                    of a dead flint giant.

Until he arrives at good cover
      the horizon-wood
            the Ashground

where he tries to avoid remembering
        thousands of bluebell bulbs
hoarding their extravagant and ravishing colour tide
        under a camouflage of wet leaves.

                    *

On the train
        immediately his father is allowed visitors
the caverns of Liverpool Street
            the brilliant moss ledges and lumps
        lighting the cindery brickwork
            might as well not exist.

Fenchurch and Stratford   Witham and Shenfield.

        Then the draggle and widening light
            above childhood flatlands
                that still bewitch him
with their marvellous corals
            and Elvis-quiffed fish
        invisible to everyone except himself.

In the surprise of this haste
            he wonders under his breath
could it be ending now
        this eternal interval with his father
            this lifetime of silence.

Throttled
    that would be one word
        for both of them as bad as each other.

Choked   he admits
by their spitting resemblance
                their
    actually rather relieving
        violent differences of opinion.

At the very idea
        a sensation like sea water
seeping through dry sand
            consumes him.

He stares off
        through the quivering carriage window.

He dreams up
        a superbly powerful blade
    say the scimitar
        Boudicca forged onto her chariot wheel
hacking down perfectly easily
    without the least tremor of resistance
        every Roman soldier track-side telegraph pole

    one-at-a-time
        one-at-a-time
            one-at-a-time
                one-at-a-time

as his train sways woozily forward
    and by magic escapes
        the snake-mess of wires
and failed conversations
        seething in his wake.

*

His eagerness flabbergasts him
                considering he cannot decide yet
                        exactly why it exists.

It even survives
                in fact it loves and guzzles
the sweaty air cocktail that envelops him
                        the second he revolves
                into the spinning lobby of St John's.

St John's the same
                where they whisked her in
from the midwinter rush-hour hullabaloo
                        and Christmas tinsel
                drooping in shop fronts

        then re-dressed her
in washed-out hospital greens
                acquainting themselves in the process
                        with her blossoming wound
                her mouth
hanging not quite

                                dead already.

                        *

He stops himself there   this time.

He concentrates instead on his father
                launching himself
                        into the old corridor maze
                                cautiously for the first few steps
                then allowing a sudden and rapid sweep forward

this way
              this way   this way
that way
                    this way

          afloat on the swirling blue linoleum
he half remembers

          taking in   sort of
hotspots where gull-nurses
                    gaggle over a titbit

          four five six
                    rigid sour yellow plastic doors

          blurred bed-row glimpses

     dozens at least dozens
                    of visitors crouched over listening
               or offering

                    a cubbyhole for Plant

a clichéd gurney
     rattling its white-as-a-sheet patient
               hell for leather
                         and a doctor in hot pursuit

before idling into a backwater
               slowed
                    like debris ushered aside from a flood rush
          to inspect
                    whether he likes it or not

a long white art gallery wall
    Yorkshire terrier   cottage garden   tabby
      Ravello   onions   sunset

before
      finally
            delivering him.

*

Ah
    but he has caught his father at a bad moment.

His father   in a chair at his own bedside
    is decked in a stylish
        but sadly only knee-length
       dark-green paisley dressing gown
peculiarly like his own
      and bowed forward with his back turned
         head to head with a doctor
       who has questions he must answer.

He tiptoes closer
    so far still invisible
      to his father at any rate.

The doctor   half his age
              flustered
    flicks him a look
through heavy black-frame Eric Morecambe glasses

      realises
         this must be a son

nods fractionally
                    and continues.

Your work   he asks his father.

        His father cannot remember.

Your middle name.

        His father cannot.

Your birthday.

        His father cannot.

Your regiment.

        His father cannot.

At which point
        he slinks forward
                until his father glimpses him
        in the fish-bowl curve of one lowered eye
turns full face
                    and smiles.

        His father knows one thing then.

And another
                it turns out.

Who is prime minister
        the doctor asks.

BLAIR

    his father spits it out
        as far as possible

BLAIR.

              *

When it is quiet again

    when they are settled
among the murmurings that pass for quiet
        in a twelve-bed ward at visiting time

he feels himself weightless and flying
    on the thermal of what he might call
            his own kindness.

But no.

    It is not kindness.

It cannot be kindness since
    it is not aware of itself.

        It simply exists.

He is a son and
    this is his father   and
        questions at least
are finally possible between them.

To prove it he asks his father
        what
        has he
        really
        forgotten.

His father raises an eyebrow
    and steers his attention off
           through the wide end-window of the ward
        to contemplate a red brick water tower
that happens to glower over the hospital hinterland
    while scratching idly with his right hand
        black beetle therapy scabs on his left arm.

    See those pigeons.

           He sees them
regular as a posting of sentries
    around the battlement of the water tower.

More than this
    his father will not say.

             *

Next day
        which is the first day
of their new existence together
    he is still in the trance
        of this new gift he was born with.

    He exerts himself with no effort
    to engage his father's mind.

He drags forward the computer screen
        on its nifty retractable arm
                until it hovers close to his father's chest
    and explains the internet.

His father will not believe
    such a thing is humanly possible.

            You
            mean
            the
            whole
            world.

He shows photographs of his children
        and a vaporous paraffin flame
trims in his father's eyes
        then flops in a cross-breeze.

He dredges and displays
    scenes from his childhood mothering dream flow
but his father was seldom there
        and will not pretend to remember.

He pulls up a different screen
                a talk-screen
    of their rare and valuable excursion
their trip in June 2004
        through the lanes of Normandy
                where his father fought after D-Day.

        Here for a moment
they do sit down together
        with sun toasting their backs

among outrageously large and bright yellow buttercups
        in the very field where Colonel Gosling
                that would be Mike Gosling
                        i/c a half-track
came face to face with a Panzer
                and

        but his father forgets

                        he presses refresh

but his father

                        he presses refresh

but his father.

                                *

                Next day and the next
        when he turns the corner into his father's ward
                and his father now bed-bound
                        rolls his marble head
                to see who   to see what
                        new interruption
                                might be approaching
        and smiles a child's innocent and complete smile
                        of recognition and relief
        he feels himself a son
                        as never before.

Airless hospital air
                composed of laborious efforts to breathe
        continues to bubble under his wings.

Next day and the next
　　　　it raises him off the clinging ground
　　　the clay that detains him.

He skims
　　　the treacherous white water linoleum
　　　　　　pathway approach.

He scans the ward
　　　　like an angel scouting the empyrean
　　　　and halts at a vantage point
where the complete panorama of the world is visible
　　　　and discovers it consists of nothing
　　　except his father here and now.

He dream-steps and descends
　　　　　to his father's blue plastic bedside chair.

He leans close to his father
　　　　like a man in a lighted room
　　　　　　pressing his face to a window
to make the outside darkness see-through
　　　　in the hood of his own head shadow.

Despite the gigantic
　　　giddying well-shaft drop
　　　　　he sees himself clearly in the depths
craning up to the moon of his own face
　　　　and his mother
　　　a smear of bridal white.

*

In the light of this
        the chair beside his father's bed
            the snub blue plastic bucket chair
with eminently breakable hollow black metal legs
        has become his one
            right place on Earth.

        Besides which
his father has decided enough is enough
    and crept   rolled
            crept   rolled
dragged himself by minute degrees
    and titanic effort
            across the interminable surface of his ice sheet
to reach the furthest coast of his bed.

    He has turned his back.

        He has confined himself to the window eye
shining in the head of the ward.

When he studies it himself
    adrift
in the almost invisible light current
        he sees as his father sees
    pigeons now and again
            slide off their water tower lookout post
                keep a precise formation
over rows of glittering dolphins
            ploughing the hospital car park
then by consent
        return as they were.

                        *

Everyone without saying a word agrees

and St John's finds him a bungalow hospice room
        closer to home
            with   as it happens
                    a flowering pink cherry
entirely filling the window frame.

And indeed
        the colour overwhelms them both

                            father
                    and son

flooding them equally with its blood pulse
                    heat illusion
canopy   and soak-through
        while the warm air they breathe together
 sways in a sea swell
                and the breeze tousles.

Not that his father has anything to say about it.

The task of breathing
                now requires his complete attention

                        and to address it

he has squared his shoulders
                and drawn himself up to attention
under the large and loose Aertex squares
            of a blue ventilated baby blanket.

            This discipline by his father
this precision

mesmerises him.

There is nothing
        he wants to hear more
                than the silence of his father's tongue

                        not to mention this other
                                new and ancient language
                lip sounds
throat sounds
                lung sounds
                                guts.

Whole hours pass
        while he is perfectly content
to trace the blurred body contours that begot him
                the shapely legs that were good for dancing
                        the well-proportioned chest
                concealing the silent heart.

He admires the long arms and nervous hands
        the jumpy hands
                that gave his father's heart away
that shook   that trembled
        that felt and showed the threat
                        of every action the world demanded
                                down to and including
                deadheading the roses.

He examines
                the sound-asleep hollowing face
                        dreaming on its pillow bank

        and discovers it more and more nearly
                        resembles his own face.

Until with no warning
no swallow   no cough
          no stir of a nervous hand

his father opens his blue eyes
               their colour astoundingly
                    faded to pale cement grey
fixes him and whispers

          never be blackmailed.

                    *

          His invincible father.

When he leaves
          he slips clean
               through the washstand mirror.

          His invincible father.

                    *

The flint village church
     where his father's coffin lies
          all service long
               in a pool of warm gules
          cast by the April sun
     through the fair breast of a window saint
the church
     blackmails the congregation.

The sexton's spade in the churchyard
    which has removed the surface grass
        in delicately snarling curls
and opened the Essex clay
           to a depth of six feet
    exposing black root-wires scrabbling for a hold
the spade
    blackmails the earth.

The priest with his swirling language of dust
    who is the first to throw   timidly
        a clutch of earth onto the far-down coffin lid
    then beckons him forward to do the same
           which he does but kneeling
               to make the fall
           and thud less dreadful
the priest
    blackmails the grave.

He backing away from the grave eyeing the sexton
    who himself eyes these proceedings
from the dark flame of an ancient yew tree
    and trampling   almost
        on the grave of his mother
he
    blackmails himself.

His mother who has waited thirty years
    for her husband to climb into the bed beside her
    and whose name has faded into the rain so long
its letters are now slivers of grey moss
his mother
    blackmails everyone.

None of which
            he thinks
    as he stumps up the incline of the village street
towards the wake in the garden of his father's cottage
                makes the slightest sense
            and will never.

PART THREE

After forty years Juliet emails him.

Can they meet.

He reads her message again   and again
          counts.

Forty years.

Since their first   last   date
          and lamplight
sweating on those oak panels in her spare bedroom
     magnolia leaves
          pat-patting a leaded window.

Four zero.

Since her slithering black hair
          creamy swimmer's shoulders
                    her big soft wide
words still fail him
          mouth.

*

He delays answering

          a minute
is hardly decent.

Very well another
            drumming his fingers
then   clickety-click at the gallop

    and   send.

                    *

St Pancras station   the Booking Office Bar
            which is her idea.

He arrives early like a fool
        giddy a bit
            thanks to his head-back stare
                at the barrel vault roof
and sunset's lilacs and charcoals
            staining the many-coloured glass.

        Or are they ghosts of the steam age?

At any rate
            he expects to kill time
            inspecting John Betjeman
                coming or going or both
                    in his flapping bronze mac
                        trainspotting the Eurostar
                    flyblown chisel-face of the future.

                    *

        But Juliet is before him.

It must be   Juliet
        trailing in one hand her overnight wheelie bag
                the other
            clamped to a mobile and why not
        husband probably
            in Paris already or wherever.

And why not.

        Except his disappointment exists
                and is frankly
        scandalous even to him.

                            *

Juliet   he remembers now
                    she told him
        is wearing dark glasses.

        Very big   black-framed
                        curved
            very dark dark glasses
        masking her face
                    as far as possible.

        That is all he has time for.

        Bye   she says.
                That is her first word.

To the phone naturally.

Bye.

As her wheels trundle to a halt.

As he imagines himself replying
            when in fact he is silent
                        and staring.

Not the white hand
            smuggling her mobile into the slit
                        of a navy overcoat pocket.

Not the beautiful black bob
            grey at the roots.

Not the mouth
            thinned under its lipstick twirl
            think of the millions of breaths
                        the words
smoking over her lips
            think of feet wearing down a threshold.

He is staring
            at scars on her face.

      Scars dicing into her lips
            little hairline fractures
                        glaze cracks
            fissures and faults
not faults no
            scars.

What happened.

      These are his first words
            after forty years.

What happened.

*

Juliet's hair shakes
blooms in a bridling pony-toss
        then soothes
                and fits neatly again.

Therefore
        he pretends he has seen nothing
                and with a bluff enthusiasm
                        which for all she knows
                is now his natural everyday manner
                steers her into the bar of the Booking Office
and round to a
                bloody miracle
                        empty corner table
        without another word spoken.

*

In their background
        departure times and destinations
                trudge through watery echoes.

In their immediate vicinity
        high-gloss woodwork   new olde England
                horse-brasses
                and everyone taking a breather.

        He follows suit.

He orders house white
        and the waitress who understands
                speed is the essence
    rattles it down
            in a profoundly nervous silvery ice bucket.

*

Juliet meanwhile
        eases her dark glasses
    a fraction along her nose
        and rests them on a pale skin-ridge
the main scar there
        to hide it.

She has no time to waste
        and without the least flourish or sidestep
            delivers a boiled-down
                recitative
namely   her life since last they met
                    and parted.

        Au pair   marriage
        two children   girls
        living in   freelance
        films   documentaries mostly.

*

He shuffles his glass on the tabletop
        creased apparently
        with ghostly cloth wipes

and cannot prevent himself
    still looking
        when he thinks she is not looking.

    At her hair sweetly hooked behind one ear.

At her jittery ear stud on its plump little flesh-cushion.

    At her white throat   very white throat
      swelling when she swallows
in the shadowy collar V
          of her expensive black silk shirt.

At her surprising   forgotten
      blunt-tipped   almost square-ended fingers
    nails unpainted   milky suns
      rising from the cuticle.

               *

Then his turn   he thinks.

    But that is not what she came for.

    She stalls him.

    She slips off her dark glasses
        and shows him her white face
naked.

               *

If she told him a wild cat
        launching out of a pine forest

if she told him a lightning strike

        a firework

an alleyway bottle-end lunge

    if she told him a particularly sharp idea
        an idea like a star birthing
            the most brilliant idea imaginable
had shattered out of her brain
                through her left cheek
        engulfed her left eye
and scorched her mouth

            he would believe her.

But   a company car
        the M40 late at night
                    darkness   rain
                and roly-poly down the embankment
outside High Wycombe

                    High
        Wycombe

    which Juliet offers
            without him asking
he cannot accept
            and must.

                    *

No sooner
the wet tarmac rubber smear
the barrier can-opened
the mud gouge   the grass rip
the steaming hush and blue dashboard glow

than his mother of course.

His mother in her own seamless flash footage
head shaved gingery bare
tiger-slash operation scar
eyes pulpy   bruise-mashed
oxygen   tank   tube   mask
oxygen itself
pressing a skeletal finger to pursed lips

sssssssssshhhhhhhhh.

*

Juliet fills her glass   his glass
but for him enough.

Enough.

If he had come with a plan.

If he had ever   and he had
he sees that now
in corn-yellow soft focus.

If he had ever imagined they might.

Then   shame on him.

Shame on him and
                    why not just creep away immediately
          with his tail and whatever else
              tucked between his legs.

                              *

Which Juliet has no time for.

      She is watching the clock.

                    She is insisting her point is not
          only the accident   her point
              is after the accident
                        she lay unconscious three days.

                              *

Midwinter fields
                    no footprint
          among flint bones
                    and bristly Essex clay lumps
no shadow
              the seething snow surface
                        opening
          and closing its lacy arms.

                              *

Unconscious Juliet continues
                    then awake but not

awake-awake   not
        herself.

More like a radio dial twiddling
picking on day one
      a French signal
and her voice speaking only French
      on day two
          her voice in English
                with a French accent
      on day three normal
her everyday voice
      beaming back to her
    from the spangling gas-warps
          of infinite deep brain space.

*

A waitress at the table adjacent
    clears cutlery like glittery fish in a handful.

He meanwhile
    sponges up what he hears.

    He wrings out Juliet's languages
      and squeezes them into his own language
  storing them
    along with the car wreck
the rain the rain the rain   the headlights
    stubbed in embankment plough.

Although   as the debris
    the confetti windscreen glass
      the smashed boxer's face fender

the car radio
   churning its exciting trash regardless
    and   in the midst of it all
Juliet's silence
  her scarred face   her unconsciousness

   as the combined weight of this
  groans
  creaks
  scrapes
  sinks
  settles
    and enters his consciousness

he reminds himself
   Juliet is not his punishment.

    Not if he chooses.

     *

At which point
  she arrives at the point
   that brought her here in the first place.

She tells him at last and suddenly
  she can remember nothing
   of her life before the accident.

She explains
   having forgotten everything herself
her sister remembered
   she knew him once.

She asks him
        what passed   please
            between them.

She is in his hands
            she says.

                    *

He straightens
            to meet Juliet's eye.

To enter her eye and drop
        through liquid green-flecked chestnut brown
    into the dead centre.

Which is prepared to believe him.

        Which is waste land.

                A cat look
    I know you   do I know you
            remind me.

                    *

He deliberates.

    He weighs her featherweight weight.

And he lets her go.

He lets her life go
        and Juliet in their time remaining
    bare faced   dressed in her wounds
            leans forward
        to catch what he has to say.